Holding onto hope

Michelle DeSantos

BookLeaf Publishing

India | USA | UK

Presentation by *BookLeaf Publishing*

Web: www.bookleafpub.com

E-mail: info@bookleafpub.com

ISBN: 9789358316636

First edition 2023

PREFACE

There once was a girl...now she's a woman.

Chaotic Hope

Chaos is the mind at times.
Confusion is our blood and bones.
Hearts holding onto hope.
Prayers needed.
Souls seeking and pleading.
And you wonder.
Watching. Waiting.
Anticipating...
How will you make it through?
Suddenly the cloud lifts.
And you feel more like you.
Chaos is the mind sometimes.
But hearts always find their hope.

-<3-
mlw

Push & Pull of the Heart

It's like a catch 22.
A vicious cycle of wanting you.

Grief and Enlightenment.
A mix of the two.

Emotions run high.
So does the pull that binds.

I talk myself into it.
I talk myself out.

Given the choice.
You walked away with no doubt.

None of it makes sense.
You did it suddenly.

And yet somehow I'm still here,
Waiting...and worrying...

-But not for long.

-<3-
mlw

Who was I?

Who was I with you?
I look back and I wish I knew.
You may have worn a mask.
Maybe I did too.
And that's how I know,
I wasn't meant for you.
Because I shouldn't have been met with fear-
After sharing something so intimate, so dear.
Nerves got the best of me.
I handed you a key.
All so you could crisp and clearly.
Walk away.

-<3-
mlw

Love light

No matter how cynical
the love light inside me
continues to beat bright
to light up the night sky
to fight for a fairytale
worthy of romance novels
and rom coms
and delight
A hope purely held
A love like nothing and with no one else

-<3-
mlw

Waves

Maybe the wave of feels are needed.
The constant confusion and then sudden clarity.
The back and forth.
The light and dark.
Day and night.
Wonder and dread.
I am all made of emotions so that I can
CREATE.
RELATE.
ARTICULATE.
NEVER HATE.
Just love and grow.
But just like a wave that crashes.
Another starts right back up again. Frothing
over.
Pushing. Pulling.
Tides flowing.
In an odd way that sound- that vision of crystal
blue- of nature- is peaceful.
Beautiful.
A beach of paradise.
An inner calm.
A religion.
A safe place to call home.
In a sea of chaos.

Growing can be a lot like breaking...
Cracking...
Splitting...
Shaking...
An attack on your comfort zone.
On everything you've ever known.
And yet it is so necessary.
To create the person God has in his heart for you
to be.
So ride the waves of life.
And always find your calm.

-<3-
mlw

My healing reckoning

Jilted and Jaded.
Never elated.
And you sit there.
And you act like it's my fault.
My sins.
My problems.
My struggles.
My anxieties.
My pain.
But my reckoning?
You haven't seen it.
Because it's quiet.
Introspected...
and healing.

-<3-
mlw

What do you want?

Do it.
Fear it.
Faith it.
Elevate it.
What do you want?
To do?
To be?
To feel?
Relationship status like a clock ticking pinwheel.
Confusion clouds.
Hazy minds and self doubt.
What do you want...
To do?
To be?
To feel?
No one can decide but you.

-<3-
mlw

Time Tick Tricks

No sense.
No sense at all.
Fear of technology.
Of disconnection.
Fear of a dropped call.
These little things.
These weird, strange stresses.
These anxieties.
These common guesses.
Of thoughts.
Predicting the future.
Or swallowing the past.
Or possibly, simply sitting in the present.
The present.
Oh what a gift.
A gift of beauty, of confusion, of tricks.
Time ticks.
The biggest trick of all.
And I sit here and wait for you to fall-
in love, with me.
This loving, happy glee.
Imagine it just coming naturally.
I could keep going.
But where would that find us.
Or break us.

Love us or leave us.
No sense.
No sense at all.
It's a mystery.
This life of living and love we lead.

-<3-
mlw

We carry tokens
in our pockets

Finding...
Pockets of Joy.
Tokens of Faith.
Lord we need you to be our saving Grace.
Stay with me.
Pray with me.
Guide me.
Never leave me, but lead me.
Amen.

-<3-
mlw

Peace prayer

Pray for peace.
In the plights of uncertainty-
in the depths of joy,
in the swirls of pain.
In the confusing days.
Pray for peace-
of mind,
of brain,
of heart,
of soul,
of world,
of galaxy.
Far away,
or nearby.
So many infinite questions-
Why?
And so we pray...to find a way.
Amen.

-<3-
mlw

Question of faith

If you don't have your faith-
then what do you have?
No really...
I'm asking.
Because, quite honestly I'm scared to think of a
world where faith doesn't exist.

-<3-
mlw

Marriage & Me

If God wants us married.
We'll meet one day soon.
It'll never be too late,
for our love story to bloom.
Age be a number.
Fear be a vice.
When God knows two souls are made for one
another-
He won't have to think twice.

-<3-
mlw

A Fantastical Being

She was late in love.
Finding and falling.
Through all the confusion-
she kept stalling.
Blink and you miss him.
Don't fall asleep.
Let your heart be open.
And your soul not weep.
For a fantastic being is right around the corner.

-<3-
mlw

Story of a painting

One with music.
His hands glide over ivory piano keys,
wearing a clean, crisp suit.
Fingers dancing magically.
And I wonder, I wish.
Those hands were on me.
Why do you think I put on this red dress?
So slinky and tight.
To enhance my curves-
it hugs me just right.
Your cologne like your song.
Mixing with my perfume.
Enchantment for days.
Our signature scent.
Gold glitter wallpaper.
Green leafy trees.
One with the music.
I wonder if he even sees me.
Standing here.
His playing of keys-
his playing of me.
Jazzy feelings running through us two.
Or so I hope-
this red dress gives you a clue.
Mark your sounds of territory.

Like this dress marks my curves.
Hiding desires in plain sight.

-<3-
mlw

*inspired by the art piece- "Enchanting Keys" by
Monica Stewart

First Heartbreak Kid

She whispered to herself.
My heart needs a break.
From you.
And what we could have been.
But I spoke too soon.
And you were less of a man.
Than I thought.
Or maybe you just got scared.
Maybe it was too much too soon.
Maybe it wasn't fair.
Should I say thank you for letting me go.
Or should I hate you, for hurting me so.
Because boy what you did.
Was my first heartbreak, kid.

-<3-
mlw

Graced by love

Clicking through pages.
Afraid to make changes.
Will I always be this way?
Will the "real" ones never stay?
What is wrong with me? I often think.
My life has flown by in a blink.
I want a love.
Graced from up above.
Is that too much to ask for?

-<3-
mlw

My Ultimate Wish

The kind of love where you know how your
person takes their coffee.
How they play with their fidget ring to pass the
time.
And talk with their hands.
How big their heart is.
And every fleck of gold in their eyes.
To know they'll always want a hug without
asking why.
How they sleep with many pillows before there
was you.
How they love to drink wine and love to eat too.
How they can write their feelings better than
they can talk.
How it's always a good time for a nature walk.
And sleeps with the tv on, for white noise and
sound.
And prays every night for a love to be found.
How she was inexperienced before all this.
But that you have always been her ultimate
wish.

-<3-
mlw

Together & Apart
(A Fairytale)

Separate we are each a work in progress.
Two parts of a whole looking for one another.
Fighting against all of life's odds.
Of constant loneliness.
But together...
We are a forever masterpiece.
The perfect end to every sentence.
The once upon a time and happily ever after.
The mate to my soul.
That may seem like a lot for some.
A lot of pressure for some.
But for us, it's undeniable poetry.
It's Love.

-<3-
mlw

Run before you get caught

That first one. That first taste. Damn, he did a
number on me. I'm sorry.
Why does rejection paint us in such poor light?
Imagine showing someone who you are.
Insecurities and fears and all.
Just to have them say you aren't what they want.
Tears late at night.
For years of loneliness.
This is my forever plight.
Talk about painful.
And so I cut it off before I can ever hurt your
heart.
Or I suppose before you can hurt mine.
Because I know what that feels like.
And if I did hurt your heart, by some chance.
I am so very sorry.
And I wish you endless happiness.
And countless beautiful memories.

-<3-
mlw

Be yourself, nobody else

Comparison is a kill joy.
The opposite of happy.
The evil to moving forward.
The black in the night.
It's hard to stay positive when you feel stuck.
Feelings are overwhelming.
Especially those concerning matters of the heart.
Comparison takes up my time.
And poisons my mind.
For we are all so different
It's a shame to let anxiety win.

-<3-
mlw

I'll allow it

Allow yourself space.
To grow.
To pace.
To feel.
To hide.
To ride the wave of life's tide.
To feel your feelings- deeply.
To find a love that is felt so sweetly.
Allow yourself time.
Though it may seem like its ticking by.
God is in charge of your timeline.
A true lifeline.
Never late.
Trust in your fate.

-<3-
mlw